"The most Powerful yet Super Simple Secrets
to raise funds on your Terms"

CRACK
THE
FUND-RAINING
CODE

Easy Hacks to Supercharge your Business

"The most Powerful yet Super Simple Secrets
to raise funds on your Terms"

CRACK
THE
FUND-RAINING
CODE

Easy Hacks to Supercharge your Business

DEEPAK PAWAR

#1 Business Finance Coach

Worldwide Publishing by

Pendown Press

Powered by G **Gullybaba**

PENDOWN PRESS
Powered by **Gullybaba Publishing House Pvt. Ltd.,**
An ISO 9001 & ISO 14001 Certified Co.,
Regd. Office: 2525/193, 1st Floor, Onkar Nagar-A, Tri Nagar,
Delhi-110035
Ph.: 09350849407, 09312235086
E-mail: info@pendownpress.com
Branch Office: 1A/2A, 20, Hari Sadan, Ansari Road,
Daryaganj, New Delhi-110002
Ph.: 011-45794768
Website: PendownPress.com

First Edition: 2021

ISBN: 978-93-91266-58-5

All Rights Reserved
All the ideas and thoughts in this book are given by the author and
he is responsible for the treatise, facts and dialogues used in this book.
He is also responsible for the used pictures and the permission to use
them in this book. Copyright of this book is reserved with the author.
The publisher does not have any responsibility for the above-mentioned
matters. No part of this publication may be reproduced, distributed,
or transmitted in any form or by any means, including photocopying,
recording, or other electronic or mechanical methods, without the
prior written permission of the publisher and author.

Layout and Cover Designed by Pendown Graphics Team
Printed and Bound in India by Thomson Press India Ltd.

Dedication

I lovingly dedicate this Book to my parents,
Smt. Sushila Pawar and Shri B. C Pawar.
The completion of this work would not have been
possible without their Love, Support, Patience
and most of all, their Blessings.

Acknowledgements

I would like to express my gratitude to the many people who saw me through this Book, to all those who provided support, talked things over, read, wrote, offered comments and assisted in the editing, proofreading and design.

Nobody has been more important to me in the pursuit of this project than the members of my family. I would like to thank my parents, whose love and guidance are with me in whatever I pursue. They are the ultimate role models.

Most importantly, I wish to thank my loving and supportive wife, Sunita Pawar, and my two wonderful children, Hiren and Yashasvi, who provide unending inspiration.

I also wish to thank my twin brother Dr. Dilip Pawar and my nephews Jatin & Jayesh, who constantly supported me throughout the Book.

I want to thank Manuj Bajaj for triggering a thought in me 1.5 years back and guiding me to write a book.

I would also like to express my gratitude and special thanks to Akshar Yadav for being a great mentor and friend to me, guiding and pushing me hard to complete the Book and make this finance knowledge readily available to everyone. I would also like to thank his amazing team members - Pankaj, Payal & Palak, for providing excellent support.

I also wish to especially thank my close friends and old colleagues in banking Arpit Chaturvedi, Kaushik Mehrotra,

Sunil Malhotra, Anuj Singh, Randhir Shyam, Ravinder Dagar, Rajiv Goyal, Manish Sharma, CA Raman Khatuwala, Rahul Parti, Vinay Aggarwal, Ujjwal Dalmia, Pradeep Jain and CA Swastik Jain for always being available for discussions on various aspects of financing and helping me to create this Book.

I am also thankful to Dinesh Verma CEO Pendown Press and his team for vital support and suggestions in evolving my idea into a book.

I cannot miss thanking all my clients whom I have served over the last so many years and who shared with me the ground realities of SME business and became the very base that encouraged me to write this Book.

Last and not least: I beg forgiveness of all those who have been with me over the course of the years and whose names I have failed to mention.

Message From The Author

A well-planned Fundraising strategy can work wonders for your business irrespective of the industry you're in, provided it is put together seamlessly and cohesively. Trust me; I talk from my own experience...

Hello, my name is Deepak Pawar. I am a Business Finance Coach, creator of the K.D.T.A framework (convert your business into a Money Making Machine), Author and an Ex-Banker, serving MSME Business owners for more than 1.5 decades.

I live and breathe Business Finance Coaching for MSME business owners daily, and my tryst with it began early on in my career as a banker with a leading Indian Bank 15 years back. Ever since then, it has never failed to impress me in guiding and helping raise funds for growing SME owners when they need it and, in return, ensure lasting relationships with my clients. I work with a single philosophy and with a strong belief that my growth is in direct relation with the growth in profits of my clients.

Being an ex-banker, I enjoy fundraising advisory through bank loans the most; and it continues to top my list on all fundraising options that deliver measurable results consistently.

Over the years, I've successfully used bank loans as one of the best fundraising options, using various tools and techniques, built out of my experience of working on the ground level very closely with thousands of SME owners and helped numerous small business owners, start-ups and entrepreneurs get more from their Bank Loans.

The journey so far has been brilliant!

If you implement the suggestions in this book, you can make a real killing and grow your business in leaps and bounds. Besides, as we often learn in the business parlance, "there is no free lunch".

So why this Book?

One, being in love with Fundraising for SME owners, it breaks my heart to see how good and successful SME owners are neither recognizing nor accepting Banks as their Business Investment Partners and are not using bank loans as an amazing business growth tool. So I want to guide the maximum number of people on to the right path.

Two, I cannot coach everyone personally due to time constraints, so this book is my gift to small business owners and start-ups that shares all the knowledge about fundraising and Bank Loans that I have learnt during my journey as a Banker and now as a #1 Business Finance Coach.

I hope these lessons will steer you to the path of success by making Bank Loans your best option to raise Growth Funds.

So without further ado, let's explore the path to grow your business and profit through the knowledge I gained about Fundraising and Bank Loans…

Your friendly #1 Business Finance Coach and
Fundraising expert

Deepak Pawar

Index

Chapter 1

Check Your Business Knowledge

Before we start the journey, let's check where you stand in terms of your Focus and Control on the Critical Business Parameters.

Allow me to ask you 5 simple questions. But, promise me that you will first write the answers in the given space on your own before seeing my version of the answer. It will be Fun.

Q1. Do you want to Increase the Turnover of your company or the Profit of your company?

Your Ans. _______________________________

____

____

Ans. The majority of my clients say that one of the most important purposes of any business, irrespective of type, size and stage of the business, is to increase the business's profit with every passing day, month or year.

Q2. What will you do to increase the profit of your company?

Your Ans. _______________________________

____

____

Ans. You will agree with me that the following are the prime options available to increase the Profit in a company:

Increase Sales

Increase Value of Finished Goods

Reduce Raw Material Cost

Reduce Operational Cost

Reduce Finance Cost

Q3. What do you think, which is the least focused option out of the above four options?

Your Ans. _______________________________

____

____

Ans. I am sure your answer would be "Finance Cost."

Now the most interesting and maybe the most difficult question!

Q4. Which is the easiest to achieve out of the above four options?

Hint: We just have to work once or maybe twice a year for the easiest option. Did you get the answer?

Your Ans. _______________________________________

____

____

Ans. Yes, you are right. Finance Cost is the easiest to reduce, adding directly to your profit without making any extra efforts or modifications in your core business.

Now the most critical question!

Q5. Then why do MSME businesses not focus on it?

Your Ans. _______________________________________

____

____

Ans. The simple answer is that they do not know how to do it and feel it is too technical to understand.

If your answer to the last question is the same as above, then it is my promise that your answer will change by the end of this book. I also promise that you will become an Expert in Fundraising and that immediately you will take action to explore how much you can reduce your Finance Cost and get it reduced.

I also promise a surprise gift for you in the last line of this book.

No cheating, do not go straight to the last line:

I have put in all my efforts to make this book as non-technical as possible, as short in length as possible and written in very simple language, keeping MSME business owners in mind.

So, let's move forward!

Chapter 2

Finance – Head of All Departments

The Role of Finance in the Success of a Business

As per my long business experience, Finance is the most important department of any business, as it gives direction, decisions and targets to other departments. Ironically, most MSME owners do not give due respect to this department and avoid it as far as possible.

One of the main reasons for this behaviour is that they see the finance and accounts department as one department and consider that its main role is to manage accounting and compliance only, with a minor role of fundraising.

I am pained every time I see this behaviour in my clients. I personally ensure first to help them understand the role and the importance of the Finance department in a successful running and growing business.

Experts say, and I also feel that Business is a Number Game and these critical numbers are provided by the Finance

Department only. Without going into great details about the importance of the Finance Department (I will cover it in another book!), for the time being, just flow with me and make me three promises:

1. Now onwards you will see Accounts and Finance as different departments

2. In the absence of any dedicated Chief Finance Officer (CFO), you will play the dual role of CEO and CFO

3. And, as CFO, you will start giving time and focus on learning and exploring the ways of reducing Finance cost

Chapter 3

The Big Question–Do I Need to Raise Funds for Business?

I have devised a very simple tool for you, just ask yourself these questions and check if you really need to raise funds for your business.

Check the following questions and mark your answers in the space given:

Q1   Does your business have a vintage of more than 3 years?

Ans.1____

____

____

Q2   Is your business steadily growing and generating profit?

Ans.2____

____

____

Q3   Do you still see massive growth opportunities in the profitability of your business?

Ans.3____

____

____

Q4   Are your profit reserves and yearly profits not sufficient enough to match the speed of business expansion?

Ans.4____

____

____

If the answer to all the above questions is YES, then you definitely need to raise fresh funds for your business.

Chapter 4

Fundraising – Options

The proper selection of the source of funds depends on many factors, but primarily it is in direct relation to the vintage and growth stage of the business.

Funds can be raised either from Internal Accruals like Profits and Reserve & Surplus or from External Sources. Internal sources generally give you a limited and slow option of business growth, so primarily external sources are used for growing the business fast.

Following are the most common options available to SME businesses to raise funds from External Sources:

1. Self-Funding (yes, it is an external source, as both owner and business are treated as a different entities)
2. Support from Friends & Relatives
3. Loan from Bank
4. Private Equity, Corporate Deposits & Other Structures
5. SME IPO

Key Factors to select the option of funding:

- Ease of raising fund

- Cost of funding

- Process hassles involved in raising fund

The following table will help SME owners in selecting the right funding option.

Source	Stage of Business	Your Ownership in Company	Ease of Availability	Cost	Amount	Compliance	Process Involved	Security
Self-Financing	Start-up	100%	Instant	Nil or Bank FD rate	Limited to personal reserve	very Low	Very Less	Nil
Friend Relatives	Start-up and Initial Stages	100%	7-15 days	Nil or Bank FD rate	Limited	Low	Very less	Verbal Assurance & Trust
Loan	Growing to Mature Stage	100%	1-3 months	2%-10% higher than bank FD rate	High but limited	Normal	Normal	Personal Guarantee & Collaterals
Private Equity, CDs, Other Structures	Growing to Mature Stage	Diluted as per agreement	9-18 months	Very High	Very large funds can be raised	High	High	Nil
IPO	Mature Stage and Further Growing	Diluted minimum 25%	12-24 months	Very High	Extremely large funds can be raised	Very High	Very High	Nil

With my long experience and going by the feedback of SME owners, the most commonly used option to raise funds in a Growing business is Loans from Bank/NBFCs.

Chapter 5

Why Bank Loan – Most common Tool of Raising Funds by SME Business

Loans

In finance, a loan is the lending of money by one or more individuals, organizations, or other entities to other individuals, organizations, etc. The recipient (i.e. the borrower) incurs a debt and is usually liable to pay interest on that debt until it is repaid and to repay the principal amount borrowed within a pre-agreed period. It may be secured or unsecured in nature, with a minimum of personal guarantee involved. It is worked under pure legal arrangement and agreement between borrower and lender.

Advantages of taking a Bank Loan:

1. The Bank credit appraisal process gives you another strong confirmation to proceed further in the growth of your business.
2. Both secured and unsecured financing is available.

3. All ranges of loan amounts are available, based on the financial strength of the borrower and the security offered

4. Interest costs are low compared to the profit margins they generate (basics of giving loans - else loan will not be sanctioned).

5. In the case of high margin but capital intensive industries, bank loans prove to be the best option to earn high profits by paying low loan interest cost.

6. It brings financial discipline in business, which otherwise would not have been taken seriously.

7. May give a little support in bad times of the business, subject to the reason and guidelines of the banks.

8. After a good duration of time with a good repayment track record, the bank may actually help in the sudden growth of business in case good opportunities are available by providing higher financing amounts.

9. Banks become a serious partner in the growth of the business by assisting in other non-financial support areas like M&A, Business advisory, and Tie-ups with their other good clients, etc.

10. No liquidation of share holding of the business. You remain 100% owner of the company.

11. The complete process of loan application to fund disbursement to the borrower is from within a few days to a maximum of a few months only.

12. Business by default carries risk, and bank loans share that risk with you, reducing your business risk. It gives an option to the borrower of not utilizing all the personal savings and reserves in business.

Chapter 6

Bank's 4 Critical Factors for Loan Approval

What does a Bank Check in your Loan Application File?

Every bank has its own criteria to analyze any loan application and, after proper due diligence, may or may not approve the loan. So, I will not go into great depths about the eligibility criteria, but as per my experience eligibility criteria of a majority of lenders primarily are base their eligibility on the 4 parameters listed below:

1. Integrity
2. Purpose
3. Amount & Repayment Capability
4. Security

Lenders analyze the loan application with these 4 parameters in mind. Let's discuss them one by one.

A. Integrity of Borrower

The prime condition of any loan is that the borrower will pay back the principal loan amount along with the agreed interest amount within the tenure and as per the agreed terms and conditions. This is called the borrower's integrity towards the lender, which is the first check of the lender.

How is it checked?

Following are the tools that all lenders generally use to check the integrity of the Borrower:

1. Checking and analyzing the track record of currently running loans
2. Reviewing and analyzing the track record of old loans through credit reports like CIBIL scores
3. Studying and analyzing the bank statements for any cheque bouncing and delays in any other liabilities
4. Performing market reference checks in the case of first-time borrowers
5. By personally meeting and interviewing the borrower to form a first-hand opinion about the borrower

B. Purpose

Many lenders have their internal guidelines for not funding specific industries or purposes.

The thumb rules are:

1. Do not fund any industry which is currently in trouble in terms of growth and profitability
2. Do not fund industries that are into illegal activities
3. Do not fund any industry having speculation activities like share trading etc.

C. Amount & Repayment Capability

After Integrity, the most crucial parameter a banker critically analyses is the borrower's repayment capability. It is to ensure that the borrower not only has sufficient current financial strength but also the future financial strength to pay all the dues on time. Both over funding and under funding to a borrower are not advisable, as it may result in default. So calculating and checking the eligible loan amount with respect to the borrower's requirement is very important for the lender.

It actually refers to the industry's financial strength and the management skills of the business entity to ensure a timely repayment.

How is it checked?

1. By performing complete due diligence and analyzing all the financial data submitted by the borrower. All the current and future incomes and expenses of the borrower are checked

2. Excess of all the income sources over all the expenses is calculated to check their repayment capability to fulfil the future liability which will arise after availing of the applied loan.

3. Finally, based on the repayment capability, the loan amount is back-calculated

D. Security

If we go by the spirit of giving a loan, the borrower is taking a loan to fulfil his current needs based on future receipts. Similarly, lenders are offering loans with the expectation of gaining profits in the form of interest. So, everything is perfect. But what if, due to any reason, the borrower is not in a position to payback? What is the safety mechanism for the lender in such a scenario? Security or collateral is a strong safety mechanism for the lenders in such a case.

How is it done?

In case of default, as per the agreed terms and conditions, the lender gets the right to go to a court of law and recover their dues by selling the collateral offered.

Common Types of collateral are as follows:

1. Personal Guarantee
2. Property
3. Future Receivables
4. Plant & Machinery
5. Inventory of Raw material, Work in progress, Finished products and any other assets of the borrower
6. Third-party guarantees

Chapter 7

Types of Bank Loans

Based on Customer Segment

1. Micro Credit

Micro credit or Micro Loans refers to very small loans ranging from Rs.1000 to Rs.50,000 and is generally given by micro finance NBFCs. It is given to very small borrowers who typically lack collateral, steady employment, or verifiable credit history. It is designed to support grass root entrepreneurship and alleviate poverty. Many recipients are illiterate and therefore unable to complete the paperwork required to get conventional loans.

2. Retail Loan

A Retail loan is a loan given to individuals or retail segments like small and mid-size businesses. It is primarily given based on the financial and collateral strength of the borrower. It includes products like Home Loan, Loan against Property, Auto Loan, Personal Loan, Consumer Loan, Education Loan, Credit Card (Yes!! Credit Card is also a loan product).

3. Corporate Loan

In simple language, loans given to big, professionally run

companies are called corporate loans. Each lender has his own definition to define the size of the business to take it under a corporate loan. Loan products include Cash Credit, Overdraft, Short Term Demand Loan, Project Loans, Machine Loans, Letter of Credit, Bank Guarantee, etc.

Based on Flow of Funds

1. **Fund Based Loans:** Actual funds are given to borrowers like CC/OD, Term Loan, Business loan, Personal Loan, etc.

2. **Non-Fund Based Loans:** No funds are given to Borrower like Letter of Credit, Bank Guarantee, etc. It is more like an assurance for some predefined commitment. In case of non-achievement of commitment, actual funds are paid to the beneficiary party, converting this loan into a fund based loan.

Based on Purpose

1. **Personal Loan:** A Personal Loan is a loan that you can take to meet unspecified individual financial needs. It can be taken for various purposes such as a wedding, travelling, paying education fees, medical emergencies or any undefined reason etc. It is unsecured in nature.

2. **Home Loan:** It is a mortgage loan used to purchase a home, construct a house, or renovate a home. It is secured in nature, and the property under purchase is mortgaged to the lender. They are supposed to be the cheapest loan products offered by banks, primarily promoted and supported by the government. There are some tax benefits also associated with home loans.

3. **Business Loan:** It is a loan given purely to meet the business requirements of a business entity. It can be

both unsecured and secured in nature. Banks are critical in analyzing and approving business loans as compared to other loans. They play a very crucial role in the growth of the economy of a country.

4. **Car Loan:** A Car loan refers to the financial product that allows someone to acquire a car. Mostly, it is given to purchase a new car and is generally offered at the car dealer point.

5. **Consumer Loan:** It refers to loans given at points-of-sale of high value personal durable goods like AC, Fridge, TV, Washing machine etc.

6. **Gold Loan:** A Loan given against your existing gold jewelry valuation is called a Gold Loan. Generally, it is the fastest way to avail of a loan from a lender. For a lender, it is supposed to be the safest way to give a loan to a borrower.

7. **Education loan:** The loan given to a student to meet education expenses (primarily fees) is called an Education loan. This loan is available for under-graduation and higher studies. Based on each bank's policy, it may be given as an unsecured loan for a smaller loan amount or against collateral for a higher loan amount. The borrower is usually expected to pay back the loan after the completion of the course.

8. **Credit Card – Yes, a Credit Card is also a loan:** A Credit Card is a payment card issued to users (cardholders) to enable them to pay for an expense made for the purchase of goods and services. The bank grants a line of credit to the cardholder, from which the cardholder can borrow money for the payment. If the outstanding amount is paid within a predefined specific

period, no interest will be charged. Else a fixed rate of interest will be charged for the delayed payment period. It is supposed to be the highest interest rate bearing product.

Based on Collateral

Secured Loan: A secured loan is a loan in which the borrower pledges some asset (e.g. property, Machine, Car, etc.) as collateral against the loan taken. The loan is thus secured against the collateral. If the borrower defaults, the creditor takes possession of the asset used as collateral and may sell it to regain some or the entire amount originally loaned to the borrower. Secured debt may attract relatively lower interest rates than unsecured debt because of the added security for the lender.

Unsecured loan: An unsecured loan is a loan that is not secured by any collateral except the general obligation. Unsecured loans are primarily sanctioned based on your past loan track record. These loans attract higher interest rates than secured debt because of the lack of security for the lender.

Based on the Tenure of the loan

Long Term Loan: Any loan given for a tenure of more than 1 year generally qualifies for a long-term loan. Term loans are a good way of quickly increasing capital. The end usage of the funds is primarily to acquire assets like houses, machines, vehicles, businesses, brands, projects, etc.

Short Term Loan: Any loan given for a tenure of less than 1 year, generally qualifies for a short-term loan. It includes loans like microfinance, working capital loans, credit cards, etc. They are suitable for sudden requirements and for bridging the gaps that occur due to delays in payments.

Chapter 8

Process of Taking a Business Loan

Loan processing involves a series of steps to ensure proper due diligence of documents and the creation of the best offer for the borrower.

Following are the general steps, which almost all the banks follow for processing a loan proposal:

1. Submission of Loan Application files to the lender as per their required list of documents. The list may vary from lender to lender, but primarily it includes

   i. Loan application form

   ii. Financial Data of the borrower

   iii. KYC (Know Your Customer) Data of entity, Owner of entity and Co-applicant (if any)

   iv. Complete detail of collateral offered, as an entire chain of property papers, details of Plant & Machinery, etc.

2. Due Diligence of data, borrower and collateral by the bank through third party field visits and investigations.

3. Bank specific approving department authorized person's visit and meeting with the borrower
4. Loan eligibility calculation based on all due diligence reports
5. Preparation and submission of the final offer by the lender to the borrower in the form of a Formal Sanction Letter.
6. Negotiation and acceptance of Sanction Letter by the borrower through signing and submitting it back to the lender
7. Entering into a loan agreement with the bank through signing the legal loan agreement documents, payments of loan processing fees and submitting the required original documents of collateral like property papers
8. Bank will perform their internal loan limit setup and pre-disbursement process
9. Finally, the bank will transfer the funds to the borrower's designated account

Chapter 9

Expenses & Charges

Whenever a loan application is processed, the bank, the borrower and the loan advisor incur expenses irrespective of whether the loan is sanctioned and disbursed or not. Accordingly, the bank charges the clients as reimbursement under various heads.

Following are the major expenses incurred during the loan processing; it may vary from Bank to Bank and from Time to Time:

1. Loan Advisory fees, if hired
2. Time and money in arranging the loan documents and preparing the loan application file
3. Loan application login fees
4. Processing fees of the bank
5. 3rd party charges for legal, due diligence of property papers
6. 3rd party charges for property valuation
7. Purchase of stamp papers
8. Expenses related to creation and registration of charges, if applicable
9. Any other charges, as per the sanctioned terms and conditions of the bank

Chapter 10

The Loan Advisor – A Friend in Need is a Friend in Deed!

In the current market scenario, financing is no more a straight-forward subject for both lender and borrower. Both entities need to safeguard their own interest while entering into a loan transaction.

For Banks, handling a large number of products, a large number of customers with multiple borrower profiles, working in wide geographical areas and working within the legal framework of the country's central bank to take care of the interest of saving and current accounts depositors, is not an easy job.

Almost all private banks and a few prominent public sector banks are taking the help of loan advisors by enrolling them as their authorized channel partners to distribute their retail loans up to the size of Rs.100 crores. It also saves them from employing an in-house costly sales and marketing workforce while simultaneously serving a large set of customers spread across a wide geography.

Similarly, for any borrower, taking a loan is both a critical and technical activity and since it is not the regular or core activity of any entity. So they prefer to hire and take the services of a good loan advisor. The prime purpose is to not only get the much-needed hand holding and expert advice but also to ensure that the complete loan process is hassle-free with the best offers as per their profile and requirement. Since a loan advisor works with multiple lenders and it is his prime job, fulfilling the above-mentioned demand of a borrower is possible for him.

Advantages of Hiring a Good Loan Advisor:

1. Loan processing is professional and technical work. Having an expert and experienced loan advisor on your side will surely help you select the best bank, the best loan product, and the best offer for yourself.

2. An experienced Loan advisor would have already spent his life in the lending business working on hundreds of different deals, dealing with multiple lenders. Thus he can give instant access not only to hundreds of loan products to choose from but also to all the possible ways of loan customization to fulfil the needs of the borrower

3. Most importantly, it saves precious time and eliminates mental pressure allowing the borrower to invest most of his time in his own area for maximum returns. Time saved is money earned.

4. Saves the borrower's money by better negotiating with the bank and seeing and avoiding any hidden charges.

5. Borrower feels at ease and can openly share all his queries and concerns before or during the loan process, which otherwise he may not have been comfortable asking a banker directly.

6. He ensures the delivery of a personalized doorstep service, saving your energy and time.

The prime role of a Loan Advisor includes:

1. To assist the prospective borrower in searching for suitable banks through his own sales team or network.
2. To present the bank products to the prospective borrower.
3. To perform the initial due diligence of the borrower, as per the bank's requirement.
4. To understand the borrower's needs and advise him on the best loan product.
5. To assist the borrower in preparing the loan application file as per the requirement of the bank.
6. To assist the borrower and the lender in the process of approving the loan application
7. To assist the borrower and the bank in negotiating and finalizing the sanction terms and conditions.
8. To assist the borrower in preparing the loan disbursement file as per the requirement of the bank.
9. To assist the lender in the final loan disbursement process, ensuring the funds are transferred to the borrower's account smoothly.

Who pays for the Service Charges of a Loan Advisor?

Lender Pays

If the lender has authorized and appointed a loan advisor, then he gets his service charges from the lender. But this kind of arrangement is not available for all the banks and all the products.

Bank payment is linked to the success of the loan, i.e. payment is done only after the loan is disbursed. So, the loan advisor also needs to invest in the loan process through his time, effort and petty expenses and is open to the risk of nil return on his investment if the loan is not disbursed.

The service Charges are dependent on the type of loan product and loan amount.

Borrower Pays

In situations where a borrower has appointed a loan advisor to assist him in the loan process, he will pay the service charges per their agreed terms and conditions.

For any borrower, taking a loan is both a critical and technical activity. Since it is not the regular or core activity of any entity, they prefer to hire and take the services of a good loan advisor. The prime purpose is to not only get the much-needed hand holding and expert advice but also to ensure that the complete loan process is hassle-free.

The service charges depend on the type of loan product, loan size, complexity, and time involved in the complete loan process. Generally, service charges are paid on a milestone basis payment model. Milestones could be Advance Service Enrollment fees, Advisory fees for finalizing loan product and file preparation, Loan Sanction, Loan Disbursement, etc. In some cases, borrowers may also ask for after disbursement services and pay extra to ensure their interest cost is as per the current market norms.

Chapter 11

Finance Cost Reduction

9 ways to reduce Finance Cost

In the last 1.5 decades, I helped thousands of borrowers meet their fund requirements and create strategies to reduce the total interest cost by 17% to 22%.

Just by focusing on the 9 simple strategies given below, SME owners can save millions worth of money, directly increasing the profit of the company

1. Do not raise Fresh Funds randomly

Yes, always first check if you really need to raise fresh funds or have you explored all the other options in business to nullify the need for raising fresh funds or reducing the fund requirement.

Savings: This is the most profitable strategy, as it may save up to 100% of your interest cost...WOW!

Case Study: One of my clients, who was in manufacturing having a turnover of Rs.147 cr. reached out to us to raise a fresh fund of Rs.2 cr. against his residential property to expand his distribution network in new locations. After the initial discussions and the analysis of his documents, we found that he had given Rs.17 cr. as credit in the market with an average credit period of more than 90 days instead of his industry norm of 45 to 60 days. This was primarily because his collection team was not very active, and there was no monitoring system in place. We advised him to focus on the collection and target those dealers who owed more than 60 days' credit. In the next 2 weeks, he was able to collect approx. Rs. 3 cr internally, not only eliminating the need of raising fresh funds of Rs.2 cr but also reducing the existing loan by Rs. 1 cr. You can imagine his savings; even at a 9% rate of interest, he saved approx. Rs.7 lacs every year. Big Saving, going directly into his pocket as pure profit.

2. Raise Fresh Funds only when you have a repayment plan in place

Whenever you are raising fresh funds from any of the available options, you must always raise it with a mindset of repaying it. Yes, even if you raise funds by infusing your own funds into the business. The most common mistake SME owners make is raising funds without a repayment plan in place. Another common and critical mistake SME owner's make is to have a repayment plan in place, but the source of repayment is not from the same business in which you have invested the money. Always check if the business for which you are raising funds is financially capable, ready & eligible for raising fresh funds; else, you may fall into a deep debt trap. Sometimes you are not ready or eligible to serve a debt. However, you still avail it, due to a decision taken emotionally (emotions are dangerous for business) or due to wrong advice by a consultant. Such a decision drastically increase your finance cost.

Savings

Using this strategy, you could save anywhere between Rs.35 lacs to few crores depending on the size of the fund you raised.

Case Study

One of my Rice Milling clients was successfully running a profitable business, but when one of his business friends entered the rice snacks business, he decided to start a new company and entered the same business out of competition or EGO. He made broad calculations that this new business would be profitable but did not focus on the cash flow and repayment calculations. He took an Rs.5 cr project loan from the bank and infused Rs. 3cr from his existing rice company as self-funding. The project commissioning took 8 months, with a delay of 3 months. It took 10 months for sales to stabilize, a delay of 7 months due to a lack of understanding of the distribution and pricing model, which was completely different from his Rice business. This resulted in extremely delayed cash flow, and he found difficulty in serving the loan repayment.

Due to this repayment pressure, he started infusing more and more money from the profits of his rice company into the new business. For some time, it went well, as now the cash flow was managed (but temporarily), and he relaxed that everything was sorted. However, this relaxation ended very soon, when he realized that there would be a massive shortage of funds in the Rice Company for the upcoming paddy procurement season. The paddy (raw material of Rice Mills) procurement season is the most critical for the rice industry as you get paddy at the lowest price. This season lasts for 3-4 months only. Every rice mill tries to store as much paddy as possible as per the plant capacity to feed the factory for the rest of the period; else, they will have to buy paddy at a higher price from the market during the off season. This vastly reduces the profitability in an already thin margin business. Now, he was left with no other option but to take more loans (Rs.4cr.) for his rice company, that too in a hurry at a very high-interest rate (11% per annum), increasing the overall finance cost and reducing the profit of the business. His accumulated extra finance cost due to this Rs. 4cr. fundraising, during the loan period (7 years) was Rs.1.77 crores (Huge!!). Above all, most of his time and energy was wasted only in managing the cash availability in both the companies.

Had he taken a decision wisely, whether to enter or not to enter into the new business, by calculating and carefully designing the repayment plan from the new company only, he would have not only saved Rs.1.77 crores of finance cost, but also would be leading a more relaxed business life.

3. Raise funds by selecting the correct fundraising option

This has been discussed in detail in the previous chapter, but still, I will highlight one of the mistakes SME businesses make unknowingly. They often raise short funds for long term usage or vice versa. It is like a slow poison, which hits you all of a sudden after a good gap, and then you have no option but to take the hit as financial losses.

Case Study

One of my good trading customers was in the business of importing and wholesale distribution of electronic items, with a decent profit margin of 5%-6%, with the volume game strategy. He was having a CC limit of Rs. 9 cr. with the bank. His OD was used as per the orders and import and based on the business cycle; his yearly average utilization was approx. 65%. During one of the lean seasons of the business, he got an excellent opportunity to buy a commercial property of Rs.5 cr. After initial due diligence of the property, he purchased it, but instead of taking a Long-Term Loan, he withdrew Rs. 3 cr. from his CC limit (during the lean period, 90% of the CC limit was unutilized) and Rs.2 cr. from his own funds. This is a classic example of using short term funds for long term assets. The negative effect of this is multifold, as it not only reduced the actual availability of CC limits in the peak period, resulting in less turnover and hence less profit during that period, but also reduced the DP (Drawing Power) limit in the next quarter from Rs.9 cr. to Rs.7 cr. It further impacted him at the time of CC limit renewal, when the bank permanently reduced the limit to Rs.7cr. based on the calculation of average inventory levels. Now his yearly average utilization of CC limits has increased from 65% to 80%, increasing the overall effective cost of funding.

The reverse example would be that you have taken a Business Term Loan even at a normal rate of interest for, say, 4 years and use it for your working capital requirements. Then irrespective of the seasonality of your business and the requirement of funds, you would be paying an interest cost on the total loan as if you have utilized the loan at a 100% level, thereby increasing the cost of finance drastically.

If you already have a loan, then the following strategy is a killer strategy and also my favourite as it keeps on generating profit for you year after year.

4. Track and Monitor the current bank interest rate

This is one of the critical roles of the finance department to keep a close eye on the rate of interest of all the running loans and to regularly track and monitor the current bank interest rates, and explore ways and means to either negotiate with your current bank or shift to another bank at a lower rate of interest. But, it should always be done based on proper effective profit calculation methods.

Savings

Through this strategy, you will be able to save anywhere between 9% to 21% of your interest cost.

Case Study

One of my clients took a Loan Against Property of Rs.16 crores, and during a period of 7 years, he shifted to 4 banks, getting his interest rate reduced every time, saving a cumulative interest cost of more than Rs.1.15 crore.

5. Keep a Healthy, Attractive, and Clean Profile

This is my ultimate dream for every client, but very few of my clients are able to benefit from this strategy. This strategy is slightly tough, but it is the most effective and permanent solution for raising funds most efficiently and effortlessly, at the lowest cost. Banks always prefer financially disciplined customers, as they come under the safest customer list of banks and always get preference. To acquire and continue with such customers, banks pursue them relentlessly and are even ready to reduce the interest cost and other financing charges at lenient terms & conditions.

Savings: No comparison

Case Study: One of my clients had a proper Finance Department with a CFO (MBA Finance) in place. He was extremely particular about all the critical parameters and the financial ratios of the balance sheet and the Profit & Loss account being maintained at the best levels. He ensured that all compliances were in place. He also maintained excellent bank communication at all levels keeping a Perfect Loan Repayment Track. Once, he was suddenly required to purchase a machine of Rs.2.5 crores. Incredibly it took only 3 days to get the required funding of Rs.1.5 crores at the best of the rates, that too without giving any extra collateral. All thanks to his clean and healthy profile.

6. An Expert is an Expert only if he Saves

Always involve an expert and professional loan advisor to guide and handhold you throughout the fundraising process.

Savings

This strategy saves 9% to 15% on finance costs and your valuable Time

Case Study

All my clients are case studies of this strategy. My next chapter is dedicated to this strategy in detail. The discussion in the next chapter will be about Loans, being the most prevalent option of fundraising for SME businesses, but it is true for other options also.

Now let's look at a few Minor but useful Strategies to reduce Finance cost

7. If your cash flow allows, always aim to reduce the financing cost by repaying the funds as early as possible. It can be done either by way of regular part payments of the principal or by making the full payment of principal before the agreed tenure. Through this strategy, you can save up to 40% of your financing cost.

8. As per the RBI Guidelines, there are no prepayment charges if a borrower is an individual and the loan is at a floating rate of interest (for exact details, please visit the RBI guidelines, as it varies from time to time). Primarily it is applicable on Home Loans and Loans against Property. So always try to take a Home Loan and Loan against Property in an individual's name without involving any firm or company as a co-applicant.

9. In the case of small working capital loan requirements, it is always preferable to take a simple Overdraft loan facility (generally known as an OD limit) instead of a Cash Credit facility (generally known as a CC limit). It saves your regular expenses like CA stock audit report, Drawing power calculation, etc., resulting in reducing your financing cost.

Chapter 12

The Secret – Get More & Grow More

Banks always look for those borrowers where repayment of both principal and interest is safe and assured. As discussed in the previous chapters, such borrowers also get excellent loans deal with lower interest rates and higher loan amounts. Borrowers get sufficient confidence for growing their business to new heights faster just because of this backup support from the banks.

One of the ways to have this reputation in banks is by prepaying your loan fast.

Ways to Pre-Pay Loan Fast:

1. Calculate your monthly profits, take care of your cash flows to meet your payments and see if there is a cash surplus available. If yes, then immediately you should use this surplus to part pay the principal of your running loans.

2. Whenever possible, for EMI based terms loans, simultaneously try to start a systematic investment plan (SIP) approximately equal to EMI. I will suggest going

for a Recurring Deposit, as they are comparatively simple and safe as compared to other SIP options. In 4-5 years, a good amount of funds will be accumulated, and you could use them to either part-pay or, in many cases, fully prepay the outstanding loan amount. If done with proper calculation and pre-planning, the borrower can save up to 40% of the financing cost. So prepay your loan fast and Get More loans further to Grow More.

Chapter 13

The Conclusion

If you have reached this page, then I must congratulate you. You are now one of the few Financially Smart & Expert Business Owners who now knows:

1. The Purpose of Business
2. Ways to Increase Profitability
3. The Role & Importance of the Finance Department
4. Ways of reducing the Finance Cost
5. Options & their comparison for raising funds for SME owners
6. In-depth knowledge of Bank Loans, which includes:

I. The Advantages of Bank Loans

II. The Types of bank loans, based on:

    i. Customer Segment

    ii. Purpose of Loan

    iii. Security Offered

    iv. Period of loan

7. When to take a loan
8. Critical factors that a bank assesses to sanction a loan
9. Documents required for taking a loan

10. Expenses involved in taking a loan
11. The Role & Advantage of hiring a Loan Consultant
12. The Secret of reducing loan interest cost
13. How to prepay loans fast

I want to especially highlight that by using this very same knowledge and highlighting the importance of the finance department, I have helped many of my SME clients by saving millions worth of money for them and arranging their growth funds when required.

Now, the same knowledge is available to you. I wish the same success for you. Your parama dharma is to grow your business and increase your profits by focusing and making the right financial and fundraising decisions.

The Gift

Making the right financial decisions may be easy for some and may not be so easy for others. So, if you feel you need further support and hand holding or have questions unanswered, feel free to avail the Free gift below:

1. A Free 60 minute Personal 1-2-1 Strategy Session (worth Rs.15,000/-)

I am more than ready to help SME owners and would be honored by becoming a part of their growth journey.

To claim your free gift, email me at **bookgift@growfs.com** with your Name, Mobile Number, location and a brief about your business and a scanned copy of the bill.

To know more about me, visit **www.deepak-pawar.com**

www.ingramcontent.com/pod-product-compliance
Lightning Source LLC
Chambersburg PA
CBHW072335150726
47998CB00017B/1144